Consulting 101 – The Basics

Dale Stubbart

Copyright 2018 by Dale Stubbart

You can find all 130+ of my books on the internet at Stubbart.com

Enjoy!

With Added Aloha

It's 2026. I now live in Hawaii. Here, *Aloha* means both *Hello* and *Goodbye*. It also means *Love* and so much more.

It's been about 10 years since I started publishing my books. So, I decided to add some Aloha to some of them. I've learned a few things since then. And, it never hurts to give a book another once-over.

Hopefully, with this extra Aloha, you'll enjoy this book even more. If you've never read it before, Enjoy!

Read on. Find out if Consulting might be the proper career path for you. It was for me.

Books by Dale Stubbart are
Like the Flight of the Swallow
Uplifting the Heart

Engaging
Well-Written
Easy to Read
Light
Decent
Different
Humorous

Consulting 101 – The Basics

Rated: G
Reading Level: 7th Grade Medium

Longest Word: Intercontinental

Consulting 101
The Basics

Table of Contents
Table of Contents 1
Dedication 4
What Does it Mean to be a Consultant? 6
    Welcome 8
    Types of Consulting Companies 11
    Consulting vs Employment 14
    Obtaining the Contract 18
    Subcontracting 21
    Project Phases 23

Starting a New Contract 26
    Day One – What's Important 28
    Day Two – Ask 32
    Security 35

Consulting 101
The Basics

    Working Hours 39
    Personal Time 44
    Attire – What to Wear 46

Travelling for Work 48

    Travel Assignments 50
    Covered Expenses 54
    Getting There and Back 58
    Lodging Options 63
    Points, Miles, Status 65
    What to Pack – The List 70
    More Things to Pack 75
    Organizing My Luggage 79
    TSA – Transportation Security Administration 83
    Food 88
    Tipping 91

Other Things to be Aware of .. 94

    Safety 96
    The Houseless 99
    Making the World a Better Place 102
    Medical Needs 104
    Allergies and Sensitivities 108

Conclusion 111

Consulting 101
The Basics

About the Author 115
    Transformational Consultant 118
    Writer, Story Teller, Author 120
    On the Outskirts of Paradise 124
    Where I and my Books are on the Web 126

Consulting 101
The Basics

Dedication

I would like to thank my uncle Gerald Thomas for getting me my first position as a Consultant for his Company – Thomas Data Systems. Little did I realize then that most of my IT Career would be as a Consultant.

I would like to thank my wife for putting up with my being gone almost every week of the year for several years on Travel Assignments when I was working as a Consultant.
I enjoyed the travel. But, I missed being with you.

I would like to thank all of the Consulting Companies and Clients who have invited me to be a part of their Team. I would especially like to thank those who invited me back multiple times.

Consulting 101
The Basics

Also, I would like to thank all of the Consultants and the Employees of the Clients who let me use them as References.

I've no doubt left someone out. Thank you, also.

Consulting 101
The Basics

<u>What Does it Mean to be a Consultant?</u>

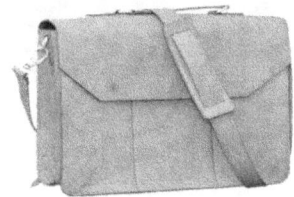

In several ways, being a Consultant is similar to being an Employee. In some important ways, however, it's different.

During my Computer Career, I've been an Employee.

My first job was at an airport maintenance company in Saudi Arabia as a Junior Programmer.

Even after I started working as a Consultant, there were times when I switched back to being an Employee of a Company.

Consulting 101
The Basics

I've also been a Consultant who worked for a Consulting Company. This was my entry into Consulting. And, it worked well for many years. Even though I was a Consultant, I was still an Employee of the Consulting Firm.

When I'm an Independent Consultant, I work for my own Company. In this case, I'm an Employee of my own Company.

Consulting 101
The Basics

Welcome

Hello. My name's Dale Stubbart. Maybe you've heard of me.

I've consulted for Individuals, Small Businesses, Non-Profits, and Fortune companies. I've been a Consultant to more than 40 different Clients.

I've consulted for companies in:
AZ, CA, CO, DC, FL,
ID, IN, IL, MI, MN,
NE, OH, PA, WA, WI,
Guam [GU],
and Toronto, Canada.

I would love to consult for companies in:
HI
The Caribbean
Europe
The Australia region
Japan

I've been in IT for over 40 years. I've been a Computer Consultant for almost as long. I've worked

Consulting 101
The Basics

for or with several Computer Consulting Companies including: Yellow Bear Journeys, Stubbart Consulting, Thomas Data Systems, Technalysis, Smith McCann, Prithibi, and Meridian. Ever heard of any of them?

What about Computer Task Group (CTG), Keane. Adecco, EP2M, Nityo, Staff Matters, Waggware, Centric Consulting, Sure Power, Select Computing? Still no?

How about HCL, Guidehouse, Accenture, Oracle, PwC (Pricewaterhouse Coopers), Oxford Global? Surely you've heard of one of them!

I've worked for or with all of those Consulting Companies and more. The point is, it doesn't matter how well known the Consulting Company is. The Basics of Consulting are still the same.

Welcome to Consulting 101 – The Basics

Yellow Bear Journeys is my own current Consulting Company. Stubbart Consulting was my previous Consulting Company. Thomas Data Systems, Technalysis, Smith McCann, and Waggware no longer exist. EP2M got bought by FivePoint which got bought by Ernst Young. The rest are still in existence as far as I know.

Five of the Consulting Companies I worked for had less than 10 Consultants. Two had less than 50. The

Consulting 101
The Basics

rest were all larger. Those included some of the largest Consulting Companies in the World.

    I consulted for one Client for almost 12 years. My average contract / project assignment lasts 10 months. My shortest contract was 1 day.

    When possible, Clients tend to offer me extensions on my contract. Sometimes, that's due to the project running longer than they expected (not my fault). However, mostly, that's because they appreciate what I bring to the Project and to the Team.

Consulting 101
The Basics

Types of Consulting Companies

There are various types of Consulting Companies: The main types, in no particular order, are:
- Management
- Business
- Strategy
- Operations
- Financial
- Technical
- IT (Computer)
- Human Resources

There are also other types of Consulting Companies:
- Energy
- Marine
- You name it

My company, Yellow Bear Journeys, is now a Transformation Consulting Company. I help people transform their lives. I help companies transform their business. I help people transform the

Consulting 101
The Basics

environments they live in. I help transform computers and books.

Consulting Companies might be one-person businesses like mine, small businesses, medium-sized businesses, large businesses, or the Big Four.

The Big Four, used to be the Big Eight. The Big Eight were the Financial Consulting Companies Arthur Andersen, Arthur Young, Coopers and Lybrand, Ernst and Whinney, Delloite Haskins and Sells, Peat Marwick Mitchell, Price Waterhouse, and Touche Ross.

Through mergers and acquisitions, the Big Eight eventually became the Big Four. (This is just the basics. So, I won't give you a thorough history lesson here.) – Ernst and Young (EY), Deloitte Touche Tohmatsu Limited (commonly known as Deloitte), KPMG, and PricewaterhouseCoopers (PwC).
Not only did the Big Eight merge with others of the Big Eight, they merged with many smaller Consulting Companies as well.
Deloitte is the largest with over 450,000 employees.

The Big Four are no longer limited to Financial Consulting. Now, they practice multiple types of consulting.

Consulting 101
The Basics

The largest Management Consulting Companies are McKinsey, Boston Consulting Group (BCG), and Bain. These are sometimes called the Big Three or MBB (for the first initial of their names). McKinsey has 40,000 employees.

The largest IT (Computer) Consulting Companies are Accenture (800,000 employees), CapGemini, Deloitte, Ernst Young, PwC.[1]

The largest Human Resource Consulting Companies are Accenture, Deloitte, Ernst and Young, Aon Hewitt, and Boston Consulting Group.[2]

It doesn't matter what *type* of Consulting Company you work for. The basics are still the same.

---

[1] **Largest IT Consulting Firms:**
https://en.wikipedia.org/wiki/List_of_IT_consulting_firms

[2] **Largest HR Consulting Firms:**
https://www.zippia.com/advice/largest-hr-consulting-firms/

Consulting 101
The Basics

Consulting vs Employment

In many ways, Consulting is similar to being employed at the Client.

The main difference is that Consultants usually start each project with a new Client. Some Consultants I know start a new project at a new Client practically every week.

My average time working for a particular Client is ten months. My longest stay was several years.

As a Consultant, there's a separation layer between yourself and the Client. This comes in handy at times when you need to be a little removed from office politics.

This also means that you may not be invited to employee functions. However, if there's a dinner or party for the project you are usually invited to that.

Consulting 101
The Basics

Some Client's have a Jeans Day. On that day, you can wear jeans, so long as you contribute to a Charity. As a Consultant, I have had to pay double for that privilege. Often, I didn't have any jeans with me. But, I still paid double and participated.

Consultants can usually use the workout room when it's available. However, that room might be reserved for just Employees.

Employees sometimes get a discount when buying lunch at the Company Cafeteria. I always have to pay full price. That's OK. When I have to travel to the Client site, I get reimbursed for my meals.

I might or might not have access to office supplies that the Client freely provides to their Employees.

I might be expected to work different hours than the Employees. Sometimes, that's good. Sometimes, it's not.

Consulting 101
The Basics

I am often expected to dress more professionally than the Employees. *Dress Casual* is usually the norm for IT Consultants like me. For Management Consultants, and perhaps for Financial Consultants, *Dress* is the norm.

In Hawaii, there's a saying, Only Lawyers wear ties. And, that's mostly true. Both Consultants and Employees can dress more casually. Often, they were a traditional Hawaiian Shirt / Blouse.

As a Consultant, I might get to travel to get to the Client. This is typically the case when the Client is in a different city than the one in which I live. I like to travel. It lets me see what life is like in different places.

I have worked remotely, sometimes for many months. But, Clients usually want all Consultants who work for them to be on site.

As a Consultant, you'll typically get a wider array of experience and learn more skills. You will be expected to become an expert more quickly or to already be the expert. There's less chance to be bored by having to do the same thing over and over again at work.

Consulting 101
The Basics

Most Consultants make more money than Employees.

On the other hand, most Employees have more paid benefits than Consultants. As an Independent Consultant, I have to paid benefits.

As I cover all of the basic aspects of Consulting in this book, I'll cover the differences between Consultants and Employees in more detail. That includes those main differences that I just mentioned and more.

If you think you might like being a Consultant, I suggest that you give it a try.

Consulting 101
The Basics

Obtaining the Contract

Before you can consult, there has to be a contract.
It's good for the Client.
It's good for the Consulting Firm.
It's good for you.

    Typically, the Client defines the parameter of the project. Then, they write that up as a Request for Proposal (RFP). After that, they alert consulting and staffing firms to the RFP.
    Consulting and staffing firms submit their bids. Those bids include resumes of Consultants for various positions and the rates the Consulting Company will charge the Client for each Consultant. Consulting Companies might propose a Team and submit an overall rate for the entire Team.
    The Client reviews the proposals and chooses their top picks from the bids. They call in the top picks, so that those companies can promote their bids.
    Then the Client decides which Consulting Company(s) to work with.

    There may be more rounds of discussion and deciding among the bids. Or, the Client can reject all of the proposals and write a different RFP. The Client

Consulting 101
The Basics

might also decide to use their own employees to perform that work.

Alternately, an Account Manager / Client Manager who works for the Consulting Company might talk directly with the Client. They might come to a work arrangement without an RFP or bid.

However, publicly held companies must submit RFP's. They must allow any consulting company to bid on them.

Sometimes, a large Consulting Company will work with a specific handful of smaller Consulting Companies who find the Consultants for them.

Figuring out who you need to talk with, to find out about contracts at a Client is an advanced art. Therefore, it is not germane to this discussion.

It's easier to find Consulting Companies to get you the contract, than it is to land the contract with the Client yourself, especially at larger firms.

Dice.com is a good place to start if you're looking for IT contracts. You might want to Google local Consulting Companies. For instance, your search terms might be *IT Consulting Companies in Hawaii*. Adding the city and type of Consulting Company into the search terms will help.

Adding *Top* or *Best* might return results from Vault or GlassDoor with the best Consulting Companies to work for. Nevertheless, don't rule out the local firms.

Consulting 101
The Basics

If you're just starting out in Consulting, consider working for a Consulting Company, rather than starting your own Company.

And, you will definitely want to put your profile on LinkedIn.

Consulting 101
The Basics

Subcontracting

I'm an independent contractor. I have my own corporation – Yellow Bear Journeys. There are two employees: I do the consulting. And, my wife advises me on the finer points. (She helps me keep my head on straight).

I usually let larger consulting / staffing firms find the contracts for me. Still, I have found some contracts on my own.

Since I have my own corporation (S-Corp), I can work on Corp-to-Corp contracts.

Some Consulting Companies have too many barriers for me to work for them on a Corp-to-Corp basis. In that case, if I really, really want the contract, I work on a W2 basis. And, I become their employee for the length of the contract / project.

Sometimes these larger contracting companies, such as Centric and Sure Power, contract me to even larger Consulting Companies such as HCL, Oracle, and PwC. Each Consulting Company, gets a portion of the money from the Client. For instance, the Client would pay Oracle, who would pay Sure Power who would pay Yellow Bear Journeys, who would pay me.

Consulting 101
The Basics

Of course, when they can, every company wants to get the full rate for having me on the project. My company, Yellow Bear Journeys still gets the same rate.

In the US, at least, contracts are frequently worked by onshore, nearshore, and offshore Consultants. (And, often, the Client also does a lot of the work on that project).

Onshore Consultants are based in the US.

Nearshore Consultants are those in Canada, Mexico, and other nearby countries or US Territories.

Offshore Consultants are those further away, usually with a larger difference between their time zone and that of the US. Offshore Consultants that work on the same projects that I do, often come from India and the Philippines.

Often an Onshore Consulting Company has a branch of that Company in an Offshore Country. The Onshore Consulting Company will often outsource work to their Offshore branch.

Consulting 101
The Basics

Project Phases
Design, Development, Testing, and Implementation

The first part of a project is called the Blueprint, Design, Project Feasibility Phase. Sometimes, it's called the Analysis Phase of the project. But, this analysis if preliminary analysis. Analysis of how to make certain parts of the project work, comes later.

A Client might work up the Blueprint.

They might create an RFP for just this piece of the contract.

Or, the Blueprint might be part of the overall project that the Consulting Company will complete (in conjunction with the Client).

The exact arrangements as to who works on what are typically worked out between the Account Manager from the Consulting Company and the Client.

After the Design is completed and approved (or more typically while the Design is being completed),

Consulting 101
The Basics

the analysis and programming work start to provide the Client what they want. Analysis and programming are considered to be the Development stage of the project.

What is developed might be something completely new for the Client.

The development might be modifications (mods) to what the Client already has.

Or, the development might switch what the Client already has to a new system or app. This is often call migration or conversion.

There is ongoing Testing. There is initial, final, in-between, and system Testing.

System Testing, tests all components of the project to ensure that they all work together. It tests to ensure that they work under a typical workload (volume testing).

When everything is ready, what has been developed is Implemented. Hardware and new apps might also be Implemented at this point.

This might be Implemented a few items at a time or all at once. How much is Implemented at one time, largely depends on how feasible it is to Implement only portions of the project and how feasible it is to Implement it all at once.

Consulting 101
The Basics

The Project Manager(s) will provide a timeline of when certain milestones of the project will be completed. Milestones are goals – these things are completed by this time.

Often the Project Manager will ask you (the Consultant) for input. That way, they can adjust the timeline as needed or adjust the number of Consultants working on the project.

Design, Development, Testing, and Implementation are known as the Project Lifecycle. In programming parlance, this is SDLC or Software Design Life Cycle. SDLC is comprised of Pre-Evaluation, Requirements, Design, Development, Implementation, and Post-Evaluation.

Consulting 101
The Basics

Starting a New Contract

Congratulations! You've been assigned to a new contract!
Well, at least, it's new for you.

After all of the excitement, you might start to wonder, What should I do? What should I wear? Who do I report to?
This section will address those and other questions.

But, first, if you're an Independent Consultant like I am, there will be lots of paperwork to fill out and complete.

Consulting 101
The Basics

Also, there will usually be reading material that you will need to go through before your first day of work on this new contract. This material will give you some idea of the purpose of this contract. It might cover some things in depth. It might focus on a particular issue that the Team needs resolved.

I read through that material. I remember lots of it. But, I really start to understand the project when I'm in that environment, even virtually, on my first day of work.

Consulting 101
The Basics

Day One – What's Important

Day One of Working on a Contract: Important People, Places, and Things to Know

At your consulting Contract or Gig, there will be an initial Contact person, hopefully. I say, *hopefully*, because I've arrived at some contracts without having been informed who to initially contact.

Before you arrive, you should find out this initial Contact's name and how to contact them. (Having both their cell phone and their email is a good idea.). You'll also want to know where and when to contact them.

You should also have contact information for someone at your Consulting Company who can get you this information. You should have that, or the name of someone on site who you can contact, in case you can't get ahold of your initial Contact person.

Consulting 101
The Basics

I try to keep as many Contacts as I can on my cell phone. That way, if I can't get ahold of one person, I can get ahold of another.

I often get helped by the security guard on duty. Yet, sometimes they need a name or at least a department to even start helping me.

It's helpful to know the name of the Client company, its address, and how to get there from where you are or from the airport or your hotel if you're traveling.

Your initial Contact person should show you around, help you get your badge, and introduce you to others on the team / project. Sometimes the initial Contact person will send you off with somebody else for the badge or introductions or whatever.

There have been times when my initial Contact person was a Security Guard who made my badge. He then contacted someone else who would take me the next part of the way.

Often, there will be a lot of introductions on Day One. You'll want to remember key people like the Project Manager.

Another key person to remember is the AA (Administrative Assistant). The AA will know how friends and family should address mail to you so that you receive it at work. They will also know who everybody is and where everything is.

Consulting 101
The Basics

Speaking of everything, make sure you find out where the restrooms are.

Find out where you'll be sitting and where breakrooms and rooms for holding private conversations are (if there are any).

Determine your expected work hours (both on-site and off).

Ask how to get set up with a laptop (if you're being provided with one). Ask how to get that laptop connected to their system.

If there's an office phone, find out the number and how to dial out. However, you'll mostly be using your cell phone for calls.

Often, the Client will have a supply room. Usually Consultants can obtain a legal pad, pens, pencils, markers, etc. there.
Often, the quantity of supplies is limited. Please take only what you need, don't hoard. If there are supplies you need which the Client doesn't have, you can sometimes put in a special request with the AA.
I tend to acquire my pens from my hotel.
Some Consulting Companies will provide your supplies.

At one Client, I needed a large wall calendar on which to figure out a training schedule. I initially looked for a software solution. However, I couldn't find

Consulting 101
The Basics

anything within the budget which would work well, not even Excel. So, I resorted to paper.

I needed something big to write on and make corrections. I went to the printing department and they produced a large calendar for me.

If this Client hadn't had a printing department, I probably would have gone to an office supply store and purchased one. I would have tried to get reimbursed for it through miscellaneous expenses.

Office type supplies are almost always available. Sometimes you have to get creative.

Also, you'll want to find out where nearby restaurants are and if there's a cafeteria on site. Perhaps, there's a lunch room where you can get coffee and possibly keep your lunch refrigerated.

Consulting 101
The Basics

Day Two – Ask
Who to Ask, What to Ask

It might be Day Two or Day Three or ..., up to about two weeks when you ask certain questions. Still, ask as soon as you need to and when it's a good time to ask. It might take you another two weeks to get answers.

When you're an Employee, your Company might assign someone to make certain that you get settled at work. When you're a Consultant at a Client site, that's less likely to be the case. It's nice when it happens. But, don't count on it.

I try to keep a mental list of who to ask what. If I don't know the answer, there's almost always somebody on site who does. You might also have a list of off-site contacts whom you can contact for help.

And, then, there's Google and various websites that you'll want to have bookmarked that will give you quick answers to your questions.

You might want to take your own laptop to work on the day you get your work laptop. That way, you can start them both up and transfer information, such as bookmarks from one to the other.

Consulting 101
The Basics

Usually electronically transferring data to a work laptop is forbidden. So, you'll have to transfer it manually (type it in). Perhaps a better alternative is to email these bookmarks to your work email (for this Client) from your personal email.

It's possible to store your data on the cloud. It might be possible to transfer it to your work laptop from there.

It's not so much what you know, but who you know.

Typically, I get introduced to at least 30 people on the first day. And, typically, there are usually 200 people working on the project that I'm working on.

That's a lot more names than my brain can take in during my first few days on the project. So, I try to learn the names of key people first. I try to associate their name with their role, with what they know, or with things I might need to ask them.

I also try to find out how I can help each person or group.

You will want to find out where on the Client's file system, the project information and data are stored. This might be in Sharepoint (mostly for documentation). It might be on the Cloud. It might be in databases. (Those might only be accessible through certain apps). And/or it might be on a server.

Then, there's the printer. More than likely, somebody will have to give you access to a printer.

Consulting 101
The Basics

They will need to give you all of the information you need to set up the printer on the laptop you're using.

The ideal setup would be if Windows could find the printer. That's never happened for me.

It's also ideal when you can just set up one generic printer for all printers. When this is the case, you can walk to one of several printers, swipe your badge, and receive your printouts.

Whether you are working on the big picture of the Project or just your little piece, it's a good idea to find out a little history about the Project, what the Client's dreams for the Project are, what the Consulting Company expects to deliver during this Project, and the basic timeline of the Project.

Consulting 101
The Basics

Security
Badges, Passwords, Data

Once, I got my security badge on Day One. I couldn't believe it! I was pleasantly shocked and amazed. And, I probably celebrated by eating some ice cream.

When I worked a one-month contract in Guam, I never got a security badge.

Usually, getting a security badge takes a week. However, I've had it take a month. In the meantime, you're usually issued a temporary badge. Since it's only temporary, usually somebody will need to escort you to and from your work area.

One Client required that security badges be worn above waist level. Often the Client will supply a lanyard (cord) that you can wear around your neck. You can attach the security badge to this lanyard.

I like to wear my security badge on a pull strap attached to my belt. This makes it easier to swipe the

Consulting 101
The Basics

badge at security checkpoints. That, of course, didn't qualify as *above my waist*.

If you want a pull strap (retracting ID card reel), you might have to supply your own. You might have to buy a package of two or three. But, it doesn't hurt to have a backup.

When I leave the office for lunch, I double check to make sure that my pull strap is attached to my belt. Then, I slip my ID card into my pocket. This ensures two things:

A) If the pull strap pops off of my belt, I don't lose my badge

B) Strangers don't find out where I'm working

I often consult with Utility companies. If people see that I work there, there used to be a possibility that they might ask me if they could give me money to pay their bill. Now, they might ask me why their rates went up.

No matter who you're working for, it's not likely that people will notice your badge and say, *Oh, I just love that place*.

This is another instance where work is best left at work.

Probably, you will be issued a user id and password. Since I work with computers, I'm often issued access

Consulting 101
The Basics

to several systems. I try to keep the user id and password the same on all of those systems.

Often there's a way to sync up all of the passwords. That way, you just have to remember one password.

When you do need different passwords on different systems, you will want to find a way to keep them both handy and secure.

You will need to change your password every one to three months – depending on the Client. Your password should be one that's easy for you to remember, yet hard for others to figure out. Of course, you probably already knew that.

The Client's data is sacrosanct, as is some information about the Client.

Basically, anything that is not already public knowledge should not be made public without the express permission of the Client. And, unless you're a marketing Consultant, chances that you will be given that permission are slim.

Depending on your level of access to the data, some of it might be hidden or masked.

Sometimes you will only be given access to test data that has nothing to do with the real world. If you see something like 99 SOMEWHERE ST or MICKEY MOUSE, more than likely, you're dealing with test data. Test data will let most people get their job done. Yet, it doesn't reveal any personal information.

Consulting 101
The Basics

When you work at a company as an Employee, similar rules apply. Often, though, some Employees are given more access than any Consultant.

Consulting 101
The Basics

Working Hours

Find out the hours that you will be working. Some Clients or Consulting Companies have key hours they expect you to be on site. Some want you to be in your seat working 24x7.

As an Employee, you might not have any choice on the hours that you work. As a Consultant, I often have some flexibility.

So, I try to be flexible about the hours that I work. Yet, there are times when I or the Consulting Company have to tell the Client the hours that I will be working, rather than letting them dictate my work hours.

I am very quick at what I do. And, I often only need to work 40 hours per week. When I'm traveling to the Client site, I usually work Monday through Thursday, 8am to 5pm. On Friday, I have to leave earlier in order to catch my flight.

I don't work on planes. So, I make up the remaining hours in the evenings from my hotel room and on Fridays after I get home.

Consulting 101
The Basics

Consulting gigs often expect you to work extended hours (more than 40 hours per week just as though you were an Employee).

I work those hours when I need to. Nevertheless, I try to keep those extra hours to a minimum.

I work a lot of data conversion contracts. Those require a lot of testing time on evenings and weekends. Again, I try to keep those extra hours to a minimum.

I also try to average everything out to a 40-hour week. So, if I'm working a long week one week, I work a shorter week the next (or previous). When that's not possible, I charge for all of my hours, if the contract allows that, rather than only 40 per week.

Since I'm an independent contractor, I'm usually allowed to charge for any extra hours that I work. If you work for a Consulting Company, they might expect you to work 60 to 80 hours per week and only charge for 40, especially when you're on a long Project.

I once worked on three separate contracts at the same time. I worked from 7 to noon on the first contract. Then, I drove to the second contract where I worked until 5. I drove to the Consulting Company where I remotely worked on the third contract for another 4 hrs. Then, I drove home. Luckily, that only lasted for a month. Still, since I got paid for every hour that I worked, the extra money was nice while it lasted.

Consulting 101
The Basics

If you work for a Consulting Company and you're not working at a Client, the Consulting Company might give you *bench time*. That is, they might pay you for showing up at the Consulting Company's Office.

When you're at the Office, you might be required to do some work while you're on the bench. That work might be designing an in-house system, making cold calls, or just helping out where you can, etc. You might take some training. I would rather work, or take some training, or ..., rather than sit around and be bored.

On the other hand, the Consulting Company might lay you off when you're between contracts. This is especially true if they're not a large Consulting Company.

There might be a limit as to how long you can be on the bench.

You might need to be below a certain pay level to be on the bench.

Being an independent contractor, I'm *unemployed* between contracts. That's a good time for R&R, possibly even a vacation. It's also a good time to pursue other avenues of making money – in my case that means taking people on Transformational Beach Walks, helping them live an eco-friendly lifestyle and/or write their book.

I also spend that time writing and publishing my books. I write HowTo, Computer, Eco-Friendly, Transformational, Food, SciFi, Fantasy, Children's,

Consulting 101
The Basics

Romance, Light-Horror, Poetry, and other types of books.

If you're going to be an Independent Consultant, it's a good idea to have six months' worth of expenses saved where you can easily get to it without paying a withdrawal penalty that's too large.

This is always a good idea whether you're an Independent Consultant or not.

While this is a good idea, it's not always doable.

When you accept a contract or are assigned to a contract, you should be told the length of the engagement. In other words, you should be told how long you'll be working on this contract. If you're not told this, ask. Typically, the engagement is for the length of the project, however long the project lasts.

Sometimes, I'm told that the project will last one year. However, I know from experience that that type of project typically lasts two years. Sometimes I'm told that the project will last three months, only to have somebody cancel the project in the middle.

Usually, you just have to take your best guess as to how long the project will last, and plan on that.

If you have a vacation planned and then get a contract which overlaps your already scheduled vacation, let people know as soon as possible when

Consulting 101
The Basics

your vacation will be. This will avoid scheduling hassles for the project down the road.

Usually, if you've scheduled your vacation before being assigned to the contract, your schedule will be honored.

I had scheduled a vacation to Hawaii in August after the project was to be completed. After adjusting the go-live date a few times, the Client and Consulting Company settled on March. I was certain it would be adjusted again to early July. I was also certain that there was no way that the Project would go beyond that date. My vacation time was safe.

During system testing, one flaw was found in the Billing System. It wasn't really a flaw. It just didn't work the way that the Client needed to have it work. The Client would have probably let it be a later modification (after go-live). Nevertheless, they couldn't alter their billing practices because their external regulators wouldn't let them do that.

The go-live date was extended again to late September. I was not on the billing team. So, I was "allowed" to go on Vacation.

I felt honored later, when I learned that they only estimated that the change would take one month, early August. Still, they extended the go-live date far enough out to allow me time to get back on site and get readjusted to work, before they went live.

That Client also scheduled go-live / implementation for a holiday weekend. But, that's another story.

Consulting 101
The Basics

Personal Time

There will be times when you need to take a personal phone call at work. When this happens, I try to go to a privacy room or an out of the way place. I sometimes walk out of the Office Building to take that call.

I try to make that call as short as possible. At the same time, I try to listen and make sure that I respond fully to the caller. As needed, I set up another time, when I won't be working, to have a longer conversation with that caller.

Many people have Facebook, Instagram, X, or whatever social media apps on their phones these days. I don't. And, I would advise Consultants who do, to only look at them when they're on a break.

Even if all of the Employees are spending time at work on Facebook, Consultants are expected to have higher standards. Consultants are also expected to set an example of good work ethics.

I've known Consultants who were let go for looking at porn during work.

Day Trading while at work, is also frowned on.

Consulting 101
The Basics

Working on your own personal projects or on work for another Client, is also taboo. When I am working on multiple contracts at the same time, I try to only work on the *off-site* project during breaks and lunch or just in the evenings when I'm not *on-site*.

Consulting 101
The Basics

Attire – What to Wear

In the old days, Consultants, including myself, were expected to wear dress clothes. For men, this meant suitcoat, white shirt and tie, and slacks. For women, this meant dress, knee-length skirt and blouse, or possibly a pantsuit.

This is still the standard for some Management Consultant Companies. It is also sometimes the standard for Project Managers, especially when they're meeting with the CEO and/or the Board.

Now, the standard for most Consultants is dress casual. For guys, slacks or dockers and a button-down shirt. For gals, nice skirt or slacks and top. No flip-flops. No shorts.

Jeans can possibly be worn on Fridays. However, you might need to contribute a dollar or two to charity to be able to wear jeans. Women can often wear sandals. It is frowned on when men wear sandals, even though my feet are just as pretty as any woman's, IMHO.

These are not my standards. I would wear jeans all the time. I would wear shorts when it's warm enough. I now live in Hawaii. Here, the men often wear a nice Hawaiian style shirt at work.

Consulting 101
The Basics

Even if the Employees all wear shorts and tee-shirts, Consultants are not supposed to for some reason.

When I'm working on a travel assignment, I'm grateful that on Fridays, I can work from home with my webcam off. I'm also grateful that I don't have to make video calls. Not all Consultants have that freedom.

Consulting 101
The Basics

Travelling for Work

Call me crazy. But, I love to travel. (Well, I did before Covid.)

When I travel, I get to experience new people, places, cultures, and languages (or at least dialects, accents, and idioms (sayings)).

Whether you love to travel or not, it's better when you can do so under your own terms.

Travel is also better when somebody else is paying for it. Many of my Consulting Engagements have been

Consulting 101
The Basics

Travel Assignments. And, somehow, the Client is able to pay both my Rate and my Expenses.

I've travelled on these assignments to Canada and Guam. I've travelled to Idaho, Nebraska, Pennsylvania, Florida, and other states.

Consulting 101
The Basics

Travel Assignments

I used to travel frequently to the Project Site. When I was on a Travel Assignment, I was reimbursed for my travel expenses.

When I receive the initial contract, I check to make certain that I will get reimbursed enough to cover my travel expenses. I also check to see that I'll get reimbursed for all of the expenses that I need covered.

It is customary that all my travel and lodging expenses are covered. There might be a limit on how much I can spend on a hotel room. There might be other exceptions.

Note: One company emailed my receipts to their Office in Romania to be verified even though I was working in the US and that Company's Headquarters are in the US.

I suppose having a different Country verify another Country's expenses might take some bias out of the verification process. It still seemed weird to me at the time. At the same time, I never had an issue with having my expenses verified.

Consulting 101
The Basics

Usually, the Consulting Company that I subcontract through wants me to travel to the Client on Monday mornings. They want me to arrive by noon and fly home after 3 pm on Thursdays. I'm supposed to work from home on Fridays.

Depending on where the Client is and where I am, this is not always feasible. I typically travel to the Client on Sundays. I leave work on Thursdays as late as possible, so that I can still arrive at home before midnight.

I sometimes fly to other places on a few weekends. That way I don't have as long of a trip. Sometimes, I do this so that I can visit other family members.

Sometimes, I just stay in town. I check out sites that I wasn't able to check out during the week (due to work).

If you fly someplace other than home, find out ahead of time if you'll be reimbursed for lodging and/or food for extra days in town. Find out if you'll have to pay for those expenses out of pocket.

Also, find out if you'll get reimbursed for your air travel. So long as it's the same or less than what it would cost to fly me home, I get reimbursed for that. The Company is still saving money.

Sometimes, the Consulting Company has a travel app / portal that they want me to use to book my travel.

Usually, since I'm an Independent Consultant, it's all up to me to book my travel. I use the airline or

Consulting 101
The Basics

hotel website to book. This usually gives me a good rate. And, I have fewer issues when I have to cancel or re-book. It's also easier to use my points when I book directly.

Sometimes I receive an all-inclusive pay rate. That means, I get paid a hopefully higher rate, but my travel expenses are not covered.

In those cases, I use a portion of that rate to cover my expenses. I could pack my lunch. However, I often buy groceries rather than eating out. (That's a personal choice.) So, packing a lunch wouldn't save me that much money.

On these assignments, I use Air-BnB to save money on lodging. However, I don't book it too far in advance. That's because the cancellation policy usually requires a one week notice, rather than the one day notice required at most hotels.

Some Consultants find a place that offers a short-term rental agreement.

When I work these assignments, I take fewer flights home. Still, I only fly with the best airlines (Alaska and Delta in my opinion). I also take public transportation, when that's available.

I have personal expenses, when I'm on a Travel Assignment, like to buy a Greeting Card for my wife.

Consulting 101
The Basics

So, I keep my personal money and credit card separate from my business money and credit card.

My wife likes to send me cards when I'm at work. If you're going to receive mail, find out how to receive mail at work (or if it's against policy). This policy can be different for letters and packages.

This is my first choice for receiving mail.

Alternatively, you can usually receive mail at your hotel. This works better if you don't want others knowing that you receive mail. Some might still notice. Yet, there will be fewer who do.

This is my second choice.

If absolutely necessary, you can rent a mailbox. However, covering that expense, and the expense of going to and from that mailbox, will be totally up to you.

I've never used this choice.

Consulting 101
The Basics

Covered Expenses
The Travel Expenses that are typically covered are:
- Transportation from your home to the Client Site and back
- Lodging
- Food

Transportation from your Lodging to the Client Site and back might also be covered.

Usually, no other expenses are covered.

Transportation
Round trip flights at the normal price (Economy or Business Class) are covered. Direct flights are usually the least expensive, but not always.

If you take a connecting flight make sure that you'll have enough time to make your connection.

The arrival time is supposed to be the time that the plane arrives at the gate. Often, it's the time that the plane lands. It seems to take forever for the plane to

Consulting 101
The Basics

taxi to the gate. Then, you have to wait a bit longer until the plane is hooked up to the gate.

You're usually not the first one off of the plane. And, you have to figure out what gate your connecting flight is at and how you'll get there. Apps help with that. You still might have to run.

Sometimes, though rarely, I've missed my connecting flight. Once or twice, I've had to find a nearby hotel to stay in overnight. That's usually covered.

I try to only fly through and to airports that I'm very familiar with. That's not always possible.

Rarely, you can get reimbursed for a rental car once you land. Usually, though, you're expected to book lodging close to the Client and walk to work. Sometimes, a rental car is provided for a group of four or five Consultants.

Sometimes, taxi's within town are covered, especially when the Consulting Company "invites" you to a group dinner. The Consulting Company will expect as many Consultants as possible to pile into the taxi. (You don't get covered for meals out that occur at the same time as group dinners.)

I've taken the bus and/or light rail before. But, usually, I find lodging much closer to the Client.

Transportation from the airport from your home and from the other airport to your lodging is routinely covered.

I live a couple of hours from the airport and my shuttle there and back is covered. I could drive and get mileage and airport parking covered instead.

Consulting 101
The Basics

However, I enjoy riding the shuttle. And, I don't like to drive.

Lodging

Lodging is covered. Usually, that means a nice room in a nice hotel.

For most traveling Consultants, the Client usually pays for Monday through Thursday night at the hotel. I arrive Sunday night. So, that's one extra night.

Still, that expense is covered. And, I might be getting the weekly rate and saving the Client money. I don't know.

If I need to work on-site during an occasional weekend, that lodging is also covered. Of course, that's less expensive than flying my home and back.

Food

Food is covered, usually based on your receipts and sometime on a per-diem basis.

Per-diem means that you get a certain amount per day to cover your food. It might mean that you're given that amount to cover your food and sundry expenses. The per-diem rate might be less on travel days.

Note: Some companies do not cover tips.

When I have to keep track of food expenses, I often keep a separate mini collapsible physical file folder

Consulting 101
The Basics

with me. I place those receipts in it each evening. It keeps those receipts and any associated notes separated by day.

Other Consultants take photos of each receipt as soon as they get the receipt.

There are other organization methods for receipts. Find the one that works for you.

Laptop for Work

Sometimes, I am provided with a laptop for work. Sometimes, I have to use my own.

I much prefer it when I don't have to use my own. That's mostly because tracking software is often installed on my laptop to make sure that I don't steal any Client information.

On the other hand, when you're given a work laptop, it might be so tightly secured that you can hardly get anything done.

Sometimes, you're tracked through your webcam. So, I shut that off.

Miscellaneous

Sometimes, cellphone bills are covered. I've never been reimbursed for mine. Then, again, I rarely use mine for work.

Often, you're expected to install email and meeting apps for work on your phone. I haven't yet.

Consulting 101
The Basics

Getting There and Back

Note: Things may have changed since I wrote this. Do yourself a favor and double check them. *Know before you go.*

Choose your Go To Airline

I try to only fly on Alaska and/or Delta. If I can't find good flights on either of those airlines, I will take United.

Some airlines offer less expensive flights. But, even when I'm working an all-inclusive rate and have to cover the cost of the flights myself, those flights might not save me money. Once they add in all of the fees, those flights sometimes cost as much or more than a flight on a more expensive airline.

IMHO, Alaska and Delta offer higher levels of service.

When I build up enough miles, I can use those to cover the price of my ticket or a portion of my ticket. However, when I buy a ticket with miles, I don't get miles for that flight.

Consulting 101
The Basics

Airline Hubs – You Can't Get Here from There

Each airline has their own hub cities. Somebody thought it would be more efficient for airlines to set up bases in various cities and to focus on flights there, rather than to provide direct flights between lots more cities.

Due to this, I can end up with the best flight from Seattle, WA to Pittsburgh, PA being a connecting flight through Atlanta, GA. (I don't think so!)

Knowing your airline's hub cities, can be useful when you need to make different arrangements at the last minute. Perhaps your flight was delayed due to the weather. Perhaps the President is coming to town. Maybe your flight was delayed due to the weather someplace else. Mechanical checks may have made your flight late. You didn't oversleep, did you?

Knowing where the hubs are will let you know where you can connect through to your final destination.

Alaska Airlines hub cities[3] are:
- Seattle, WA (#1)

---

[3] **Alaska Airlines Hub Cities:** https://news.alaskaair.com/destinations/alaska-airlines-bolsters-service-from-anchorage-and-portland-with-seven-new-routes-including-nonstop-flights-to-boston-jackson-hole-and-four-washington-state-cities/

Consulting 101
The Basics

- Honolulu, HI
- Portland, OR
- Anchorage, AK
- Los Angeles, CA
- San Diego, CA
- San Francisco, CA

Note: Alaska Airlines also has several direct flights.

Delta's hub cities[4] are:
- Atlanta, GA (#1)
- Boston, MA
- Detroit, OH – **Note:** I can hardly ever catch my connecting flight in Detroit.
- Los Angeles, CA
- Minneapolis, MN
- New York, NY JFK
- New York, NY La Guardia
- Salt Lake City, UT
- Seattle, WA

Connecting Flights

Connecting flights take extra time. I try to take direct flights when possible. If it's a longer flight or if I'm on vacation, connecting flights are not such a big deal.

Connecting flights can even be advantageous for restroom breaks. That's especially the case when I

---

[4] **Delta's Hub Cities:**
https://en.wikipedia.org/wiki/Delta_Air_Lines

Consulting 101
The Basics

have a window seat on my flight and the rest of my row is sleeping.

When I'm traveling every week, connecting flights are not so much fun, even when I'm earning extra miles / points by doing so.

A Consultant friend of mine thought about taking connecting flights to build up his miles with a certain airline. I don't know if he ever did that or not.

Taking Ground Transportation instead

When your destination is a smaller city, sometimes it's easier and/or less expensive to fly to a larger city and then drive or catch a shuttle to the smaller city. If a shuttle is not available, perhaps a taxi or ride-share is.

Example #1: If Madison, WI is your final destination, fly to Milwaukee. Then, drive to Madison.

Example #2: There are direct flights from Seattle to Tucson, AZ on Alaska. If I'm heading to Tucson from someplace else, it's easier to fly to Phoenix and catch the shuttle to Tucson. This particular shuttle is a little crowded. So, be ready to bump shoulders.

Example #3: I worked in a northern suburb of Toronto for one contract. I could have flown from Seattle to Toronto Pearson and then caught a connecting flight which would have gotten me closer to my destination.

Consulting 101
The Basics

That flight would have been out of my pocket. (I didn't check that all my expenses would be covered before I signed that particular contract.) So, I opted for the two-hour bus ride. The bus was always fairly empty. It got me to within five miles of where I was staying, for just $5.

At that point, I caught the local city bus which pretty much took me to my door.

It would have taken me at least two hours just to catch the connecting flight, not to mention the flight time.

Consulting 101
The Basics

Lodging Options

Most of the time I book my lodging at a major hotel. However, in Orlando, Florida I found a Bed and Breakfast (B&B) within the dollar limit that the Consulting Company would approve.

This B&B was three blocks from work and served free breakfast. It was on the edge of a downtown / residential district, on the residential side.

The moment I was there, I felt like I was no longer in the downtown / skyscraper district. I felt at home. I felt like I was in Paradise.

And, I was willing to trade hotel points for Paradise.

When I'm working an all-inclusive rate, I book airbnb. Otherwise, I stick to Marriott, Hilton, or Starwood (SPG), unless I can find a little piece of Paradise like that one in Orlando.

Note: airbnb doesn't really exist here in Hawaii. The Island of Oahu (Honolulu County), has a three-month minimum rent period other than hotels,

Consulting 101
The Basics

resorts, and a very few pre-approved places. Some of the other islands have longer minimum rental times.

That doesn't mean that lodging here isn't advertised in airbnb. Some of that is OK because somebody's renting a room or a condo that is in Waikiki or some other designated resort area. Most of it, though, is illegal and consists of a van with a bed and back.

I've considered renting an apartment. However, finding a furnished apartment on a month-to-month rate in a downtown area, is very hard to do.

I did rent a condo once. That worked fine.

Once, I tried staying in an intentional Community. That didn't work so well.

At the Community, I was expected to participate heavily in the Community. That might have been OK. But, after my work day, I just wanted time for myself.

There weren't enough hours in the day to participate that much in the Community and also get my work done. Plus, I might have to log in and work from the Community without much prior notice.

Consulting 101
The Basics

Points, Miles, Status
Your Status with an Airline and Where to Sit.

When I'm traveling for a project, I try to stick with one of my favorite airlines until I've gotten a good status with that airline. Then, I'll switch to my other favorite airline.

That way, I can attain a good upgrade status with both airlines.

In hind-sight, if I had stuck with the same Airline, I might have earned an even higher status than I did.

Alaska Airlines has the following statuses:
- MVP
- MVP Gold
- MVP Gold 75K
- Million Miler

Alaska Airlines doesn't have that many first-class seats on their flights. When I have MVP Gold 75K, I occasionally get upgraded to first-class. Most of the time I'm awarded or can book a Business Class flight at no extra cost.

Consulting 101
The Basics

The Delta Medallion plan includes:
- Silver
- Gold
- Platinum
- Diamond

Fliers with Delta Diamond status are almost always awarded a first-class upgrade. When I have Gold status I'm usually upgraded to Business Class.

Business Class, in my opinion, is almost as good as First Class, perhaps better. The First Class seats are a bit larger. And, you almost always get a full meal.

But. my meals are reimbursed. Or, I get a per-diem to cover them.

I enjoy a good conversation. People in Business Class are more likely to want to talk than those in First Class.

Still, most Consultants and Business People who fly don't like to talk. They would rather watch a movie, play a game on their phone / tablet, or possibly read a book. They did all of their talking for the week when they were at work.

I also like to nap on the plane. In First Class the Flight Attendant is always bringing you food or filling your drink.

That's nice. But, there ends up being not so much time to nap. That usually doesn't prevent me from doing so. I just have to time my naps differently than I do in Business Class.

Consulting 101
The Basics

Some Consultants always purchase First Class seats. Or, they purchase First Class seats until they've gotten their upgrade status. The more expensive the ticket, the more miles are awarded. So, purchasing First Class tickets means that you earn miles more quickly.

Of course, they have to pay the difference between the First Class ticket price and the regular ticket price.

The same logic and rules apply to purchasing a Business Class seat. Though, you'll build points less quickly.

FYI: The last time I flew on a regular basis, there airline was always selling First Class and Business Class Seats at a discount when you were at your gate.

Hotel Points

Each airline has arrangements with various hotels. So you can earn more miles by staying at their preferred hotels. Or, you might want to keep your hotel points for free nights and room upgrades at your hotel. Sometimes points apply to both airline and hotel chain. So, I've heard.

Alaska is partners with:
- Marriott
- Hilton
- Starwood
- Best Western
- Choice

Consulting 101
The Basics

- Coast
- Fairmont
- Intercontinental
- La Quinta
- Rocketmiles
- Westmark

Delta is partners with:
- Marriott
- Hilton
- Starwood
- airbnb
- Intercontinental
- Carlson Rezidor
- Le Club Accor
- Hyatt
- Langham
- Millennium
- Shangri-La
- World Hotels

Rental Car Points

You can sometimes earn airline miles for car rental. Some Consultants will rent a car, even when they aren't getting reimbursed for it. Rental Car points can be used for car upgrades.

Consulting 101
The Basics

Credit Card Points

The other way to achieve upgrade status faster is to apply for a credit card. Airlines offer credit cards, as do hotel chains.

You used to need to spend around $3,000 on the card before you gain the upgrade status. I don't know what that amount is now.

Airlines run promotions where flight attendants will hand out application forms, if you want their credit card. If you turn them in to a flight attendant before you leave the plane, you earn a few extra miles.

I don't do that because you have to put personal information on the application. There's too much chance for it to fall into the wrong hands or to be seen by the wrong eyes.

I'll take my chances and the lesser amount of miles. I'll fill out my application online.

Consulting 101
The Basics

What to Pack – The List

This is the main list of what I take with me. The more miscellaneous items or less necessary items are in the next chapter.

I take what works for me. Take what works for you.

Clothes

I pack clothes for the week – enough to get by and perhaps just a little bit extra – just in case. That way I have clothes for evenings, if I want. Whatever I'm wearing on the flight there or back, I only have to pack one way. That saves me a little space in my luggage.

Some Consultants pack workout clothes.
Some pack swimwear.
I take flip-flops.

Sometimes, rolling my clothes results in less wrinkles and takes less space. Sometimes it results in more wrinkles and/or takes more space.

Consulting 101
The Basics

If I'm staying in an airbnb, I take a travel iron, just in case. Usually there is an iron available at airbnbs. Where it is, might not be obvious.

An iron is usually available in your room. And, where it is obvious at major hotels. If you can't find it, ask at the Front Desk.

I take a needle and thread – just in case. However, you can usually find somebody at work who has them. You can also usually get them from the hotel. I just like to be certain I have these with me, in case.

Personal Products – Things to Keep you Clean

I pack soap, deodorant, etc. You'll have your own list of those items.

Major hotels provide body cleanser. However, that's always so fragranced that I wouldn't be able to stand myself if I used it.

Major hotels also provide hair dryers and shower caps. And, you can usually get a toothbrush and toothpaste at the front desk for the asking. If you ask and they say, *No*, they'll usually offer to let you buy them.

Consulting 101
The Basics

Computer, Etc.

I take both my laptop and the work laptop (when those are separate). I take all the necessary power and connecting chords, and a mouse.

If I'm using my laptop for work, I take a flash drive that has my personal documents on it.

If there's room in my luggage, I take a separate external keyboard that I leave at the hotel office during the weekend. I also leave other things at the hotel office that I don't want to tote back and forth every weekend.

I take my fob (if I've been issued one for remote access) and my security badge.

And, I take my notes and a notebook, pens, etc.

Of course, I take my cellphone and charger. I make certain that my phone is fully charged before I leave the house. I check that again before I leave for work on Thursday (flight day).

I used to take a watch with me. Yes, I know, I had my phone. Still, I liked to also have a watch handy. Plus, my watch easily showed me the time in two separate time zones.

I could have done that with my phone. But, I couldn't be bothered to figure that out.

Now, that watch has been gone for a long time. And, I've figured out the time zone thing on my phone. So, I only take my phone.

Consulting 101
The Basics

Back in the day, I used to sometimes take my hotspot and its charger. I would only take my hotspot when I wasn't certain of the quality and consistency of the hotel's Wi-Fi. Any major hotel has decent Wi-Fi.

Sometimes, I've had to pay extra or have status to use Wi-Fi outside of the lobby area.

Now, I use my cellphone when I need a hotspot.

When I know that there's a wired connection, I take an ethernet cable and a J5Create connection to take advantage of that. Sometimes, the hotel will provide an ethernet cable, if you ask nicely. Though with most people preferring wireless these days, that's probably less likely.

I prefer a wired connection. It's faster and more secure.

Money

I take two wallets, one for personal purchases, one for business. I take some small bills for tip money. Though, now, I can usually put the tip on my credit card. Still, if the company isn't reimbursing my tips, I'll tip with cash.

I take my receipt organizer.

ID

I need my Driver's License to fly. If I drive, I'll also need it. So, I take that with me.

Consulting 101
The Basics

My boarding pass is on my phone. I can print an extra copy at the airport. Some airports used to not have good Wi-Fi reception. So, a printed copy was a good idea. It might still be a good idea.

Some airlines have kiosks where you can print a copy of your ticket. And, you can always get a printed copy at the airline desk, provided you can get to the front of that line.

If you print a copy of your boarding pass at home, make sure that the print quality is decent enough. If it doesn't scan properly when you get to the front of the TSA line, you'll have to go back and get a copy at a kiosk. Then, you'll have to start again at the back of the line. You'll have to get a copy of your boarding pass, unless you have it on your phone and can use that version.

I also take business cards. Who knows? Some restaurant might have a bowl for business cards where I can try to win a free meal or at least a bagel.

Consulting 101
The Basics

More Things to Pack
Headphones and Earplugs
Headphones help me focus. They also let me watch a movie on the plane without disturbing those around me. Airlines often give away free headphone. Or, they might charge you a few dollars for them.

Earplugs help me sleep in a noisy hotel.

Something to Keep Me Occupied while En Route
I take a book or two to read and a puzzle book to work on. These are for times on the airplane when I can't find anybody who wants to talk and I can't sleep.

Yes, I could read an e-book on my phone or my computer. Still, I would much rather read a paperback version.

One time, I sat next to a couple who were afraid that they'd be bored on a five-hour flight. They were greatly relieved when they found out they could watch TV shows for free through their phone.

Consulting 101
The Basics

They were still greatly relieved, even after they found out the only free shows were on the Food Channel.

Sometimes I'll find a movie I want to watch. Or, I'll read the airline magazine and attempt to work the puzzles there – provided I didn't just do that on my previous flight.

Personal Temperature Control
I take my personal fan plus its charger. This is a chargeable fan that's about the size of a large cell phone.
Depending on my work situation, I might also take a mini clip-on fan.

Bags for my Purchases
I take a couple of reusable grocery bags. That way, I don't end up with too many plastic bags.
In many places in the US, grocery stores will charge you a $0.05-$0.10 for a plastic bag. It's the state law.
That charge is not high. I'm mostly using the reusable grocery bag to help the environment.

I take a hot-cold bag. This keep things hot or cold on the way home from the grocery. Sometimes, a hot-cold bag all I need to take for a grocery bag.

Consulting 101
The Basics

Even if you're not buying groceries, you might be purchasing other things. And, a reusable bag might come in handy then.

Raingear

I take a collapsible umbrella and whatever other outerwear I might need. It's not that I mind a walk in the rain. However, being soaked and dripping all over the floor and soaking your seat cushion is frowned on at many Clients, not to mention in my home.

Stuff for Writing Letters

I take postage stamps, in case I want to send my wife a card. I take stamps for letters from both my personal and business stashes, just in case.

I also take a couple of envelopes.

Clean Drinking Water

I fill my metal water bottle with purified water and take it with me. If there's still water in it when I get to the hotel, I quickly dump it down a bathroom sink before I go through the TSA line.

I take a water bottle and a filter. My filter is a *Sawyer Squeeze*. Alternatively, you could use a filter straw which would take even less room in your now slightly bulging luggage.

Consulting 101
The Basics

I could just buy water in a plastic bottle. And, sometimes, I have to. But, microplastics that dissolve from those bottles are a problem.

Eyewear
I wear different eye-glass prescriptions for close work and distance. I take both pairs of glasses in their protective cases.

Occasionally, I take fit-over sunglasses.

Last, but not least, when my wife can't come along, I take Nelville, my plush pet baby bigfoot. I don't like to travel alone.

Consulting 101
The Basics

Organizing My Luggage

I manage to get all of that into two small carry-ons. It takes a knack which I learned from the best packer in the world – my dad. You can read more about that in my book <u>Packing Petite</u>.

Make your list. Pare it down a few times. If you end up needing something once you've arrived, you can usually purchase it at your destination.

Sometimes you're given a locking desk drawer at work where you can safely leave things. I wouldn't count on having a locking desk drawer at work, at least not a very big one.

I sometimes leave a suitcase with the hotel front desk when I have stuff that I don't need to tote back and forth all the time.

Take your time to figure out what works best for you. However, you don't want to take too much time. And, you don't want to take too little figuring that out.

Consulting 101
The Basics

I have a separate little bag that contains earphones, a pen, a spoon and a fork, an eyeglass cleaning cloth, and other odds and ends.

That bag also used to hold my carbon face mask. I used to take that along to filter out fragrances in order to be able to breathe more easily,

Then, COVID came along. I now wear my carbon face mask around my neck. That way I can quickly pull it over my mouth and nose when I'm feeling vulnerable to germs. I also wear it when I have a cough.

This small bag is big enough that I can stick my cellphone in it. I keep it in my luggage where I can easily pull it out. Then, I stick it into my seat pocket on the airplane.

This little bag is a bright color. That way, I won't forget it. It's small so it fits in the seat pocket of the airplane. It's long enough that I can see it when it's in that seat pocket. And, it contains everything I might need easy access to once I'm in my airplane seat.

Actually, this little bag is a cloth pencil holder. But, don't tell anybody.

I take luggage straps in case I get tired of carrying my carry-ons with my hands.

I did carry luggage tags for a while so that I could identify my luggage without opening it. However, I

Consulting 101
The Basics

figured out that the long white paper tag, which the airlines place around my luggage handle, has my name on it. I just need to know where to look. That way, I can see it quickly and stick the luggage back on the conveyor belt, if it turns out not to be mine.

I was glad when I learned that, because my luggage tags kept getting ripped off of my luggage.

I tried putting stickers on my luggage, but they kept coming unstuck. I still take smiley face stickers with me. They come in handy sometimes.

There are times when I just can't carry one of my carry-ons any longer, even when I'm using a luggage strap. At those times, I let the airline carry the slightly larger one for me. I hand it over to them at the gate when they mention that they're looking for more bags to stow.

My smaller bag has my laptop in it. So, I don't have to worry about accidentally stowing my laptop.

FYI, in case you don't already know, the airline app on your phone will send you a notification when your luggage is on the conveyor belt. Probably, all airline apps do this now. It was a new thing back in the day.

Yet, even when you know that your bag has just arrived, if it looks like all the other bags, it will take you a while to find it.

Consulting 101
The Basics

I knew there was a reason why I was carrying those luggage tags back and forth with me. Still, if they're packed in my luggage, they're doing me absolutely no good.

Consulting 101
The Basics

TSA – Transportation Security Administration

If you're flying in the US, you'll need to go through TSA security lines, unless perhaps you have your own private jet or are flying on Air Force One. TSA lines are usually long and usually take up to two hours to get through.

If you have preferred status or are flying first class, there are sometimes shorter lines. MyTSA is the TSA's app to check wait times.

There are also expedited lines for TSA Precheck. You may be awarded TSA Precheck on your boarding pass if you participate in a TSA Trusted Traveler Program. Participating in these programs greatly increases the likelihood of being awarded TSA Precheck. But it's not guaranteed.

Alternatively, you might randomly receive TSA Precheck, even if you don't participate in one of these programs.

Clear offers TSA Precheck. Those lines can be much shorter. Clear uses facial recognition to verify that you are you. It's still TSA Precheck.

Consulting 101
The Basics

Whether you're in an expedited line or not, you can save time by being prepared. Dump the contents of your pockets (except your ID and boarding pass) into your luggage. I like to take a locking plastic bag to dump this stuff into. That way, I can easily retrieve it later without really digging for it.

If you're wearing a belt, remove it.

If you don't have TSA Precheck, or if your shoes have metal in them, remove them. This rule does not apply if you're younger than 13 or older than 74.

To participate in a Trusted Traveler Program like TSA Precheck or Clear combined with TSA Precheck, you need to fill out an online application, pay a fee, and pass an in-person interview.

After you've filled out the application and submitted it, the TSA will do an extensive background check on you – this includes checking family and friends. I figure they already know all this information, so why not?

Clear does their own check, probably in addition to a TSA check.

If the TSA thinks that you are not a threat, they will let you know. Then, they'll ask you to schedule an interview. During that interview, they will verify some information. This interview is usually held at an airport.

Once you pass the interview, they'll mail you a card. But they'll start awarding TSA Precheck right away.

Consulting 101
The Basics

I don't know Clear's procedure. It wasn't available when I first applied for TSA Precheck. And, it costs what TSA Precheck costs, plus more.

TSA offers four Trusted Traveler Programs
TSA Pre
Global Entry (GOES)
Nexus, and
Sentri

TSA Pre only gives you the precheck status.
Global Entry expedites border crossings at US borders whether that's a land border or an airport. Global Entry includes TSA Pre.
Nexus includes Global Entry, but the expedited border crossings are limited to Canada.
Sentri includes Global Entry and TSA Pre.

To tell which Trusted Traveler Program is best for you, use the TSA Interactive Program Selector. https://www.dhs.gov/trusted-traveler-programs#.
That website says TSA Pre is best for domestic travel.
Global Entry is best for international travel.
Nexus is best for frequent travel between the US and Canada.
Sentri is best for frequent travel into the US from Mexico.

Clear offers these programs:

Consulting 101
The Basics

Clear+ bundles Clear with TSA Pre. Just apply to Clear and they'll take care of creating and submitting your TSA Pre application.

Clear offers add-ons to Clear+

Friends and Family reduced rate. Though, you're paying extra for each person. So, it's only a discount on their application.

Clear Concierge provides an Ambassador to guide you through the airport.

If you're flying, you will need a picture ID. Driver's license or State ID will do. TSA wants all states to comply with RealID. RealID IDs have a star in the upper right-hand area.

TSA now charges extra for flying without a RealID ID. But, you can use your Passport as your ID, instead.

TSA limits what can be carried on planes.
- Nothing hazardous
- Guns must be checked
- Carry-on liquids must be in 3oz / 88 ml or smaller containers. Those containers must all fit into one locking quart-size / 0.9 liter clear plastic bag.

At the Seattle airport some guy announces,

Consulting 101
The Basics

Hi, this is so-and-so. The TSA has limited what you can carry on. Please check with your airline for further information.

This always struck me weird. Why should I check with my airline when the TSA is limiting what I can carry on to the airplane?

Apparently, TSA has different arrangements with each airline. Those arrangements are all pretty much the same. Still, there might be minor variations.

So-and-so was a name I didn't recognize. I figured he might be the head of the TSA.

I googled the name, only to find images of some guy who wasn't wearing a shirt. Turns out he's a country singer.

I guess someone at the Seattle airport thinks that country singer is well known.

Consulting 101
The Basics

Food

Whether you're traveling to work or not, you will still need to eat. I like to find out if there's a cafeteria on site, where nearby restaurants are, as well as where nearby food trucks and grocery stores are. If Google fails to tell you this, ask the locals.

Sometimes, Consultants get employee rates at the cafeteria, sometimes they get a discount, sometimes not. Still, the cafeteria is often the least expensive place to eat. Going to the cafeteria usually takes the least time when you need to catch something quickly and then get back to work.

I try not to make a habit of taking short lunch breaks. Hour long lunch breaks help me rejuvenate. Plus, I often figure out the answer to one or two issues while I'm eating.

I usually try to get further away from work than the cafeteria for lunch. Also, sometimes if you eat in the

Consulting 101
The Basics

cafeteria, you can get called into an impromptu meeting that's being held there.

It's difficult to stay on a diet when traveling for work. This is why I regularly visit grocery stores. It's even difficult to stay on a diet when you eat lunch out occasionally. I find it helpful to let people, especially the server, know that I'm on a diet, when I'm on a diet.

I don't like to eat alone. Yet, often my food requirements and wants are not the same as other team members who like to eat lunch out. So, I try to eat out with those team members once or twice a week. I reserve a few days where I can eat what I want, going by myself if I have to. I can also use those lunchtimes, if I just need some *alone* time for a change.

That's not always the case. Sometimes, there are other team members who I like to eat with who are willing to eat at places that I can eat at. Sometimes, I have lunch with them every day that I'm on site.

There are smartphone apps to help you locate particular types of food: Organic, Ice Cream, Pizza, Vegetarian, Steak, Local, Oriental, Mexican, etc. Or, you can search Google.

Consulting 101
The Basics

However, these apps and Google might not be up-to-date. It's best to ask the locals.

Even so, sometimes I just like to explore and see what I can find.

Sometimes restaurants are tucked away in buildings with no exterior sign letting you know of their existence. And, even, when you know that a restaurant is located in a particular building, it might be a maze to try and find it.

Once again, asking locals might reveal where these hidden gems are. If you're not an extrovert, find some friends to eat lunch with who are. They're usually happy to chat with the locals and find out where the good places to eat are.

Hotels usually provide coffee service in your room – that means something to heat the water in, plus coffee grounds, sweetener, and creamer.

Sometimes the hotels provide tea. Even when they do, I often have to ask for it at the front desk.

Consulting 101
The Basics

Tipping

Tipping is a personal choice. Still, it is wise to tip generously. I get much better service when I do. It also gives me a better chance to get acquainted with those who are providing those services.

15% tip is standard for restaurants. 10% if you have to serve yourself. 20% is more generous and easier to figure out – multiply by 2 and divide by 10. There are cellphone apps, including the *built-in* calculator app, that will help you figure out the tip when your mind goes blank and you can't do the math in your head.

The Taxi tipping standard is 15%. 20% is more generous. Most taxis have a payment platform that lets you easily choose 10, 15, 18, 20, 25 percent tip. Or, at least, they used to.

I try to carry enough cash for the taxi, in case I get one which only has a credit card impression machine. Those machines keep a paper copy of my credit card

Consulting 101
The Basics

number. When I hit that snag, I try not to take that brand of taxi again.

Now, I take Uber or Lyft or the local car sharing company. I prefer them in the reverse order. However, I might not have the local app installed on my phone and Uber is more likely to be available.

I don't like my room in the hotel disturbed during the week while I'm there. So, I hang out the do not disturb sign. Since my room is only cleaned once / stay, I only tip once / stay or once / week if my stay is longer than one week.

Standard tip is $2 to $3. More generous is $5. It might be more these days.

I also try not to leave too big of a mess in my room. If that's not possible, I tip more.

I also tip more if that hotel has provided me with special services – concierge services, for instance.

Shuttle tipping standard is 10% for long-distance shuttles, $1 for short-distance shuttles. At least, it used to be.

If the driver is loading / unloading your bags, a dollar or two per bag is standard. Same goes for taxi drivers when you have more than a couple of suitcases.

Some short-distance shuttles don't accept tips.

Consulting 101
The Basics

I know of a church that holds a week-long conference in the same city once every four years. Church members come from all over the World to attend.

Servers at restaurants in that city hate working that week. The church members flood the restaurants. But, they leave paltry (substandard) tips. Most of the church members rarely eat out and many spend what little they have just to come and participate in the conference. The church has a cafeteria that is always more than crowded. So, if they want to eat, many of the attendees have to eat out.
The best servers in town do not work that week. Those who do, might end up earning less in tips for the week. The locals who often tip better, stay home to avoid the crowds.
Not only do the servers hate that week, they end up hating the church and its members.

When you're a consultant you represent yourself, your Consulting Company, and the Client. It's always wise to leave a good impression.

Consulting 101
The Basics

Other Things to be Aware of

There's a lot more to know about the Project that you will be working on. Yet, each Project is different enough, that you'll need to learn much of that on the job.

There's also more to know about the Contract. But, most contracts are similar. And, if you're working for a Consulting Company, you can let them take care of most of the Contract details.

In this section, I'll cover a few more things that most Projects have in common regarding Safety, The Houseless, and Medical Needs. These might apply

Consulting 101
The Basics

more to Travel Assignments. Yet, they're still applicable to most Projects.

Consulting 101
The Basics

Safety

Try to keep yourself safe. If you're lodging, working, commuting, or for some other reason are in an unfamiliar neighborhood, learn which areas are safe. There's safety in numbers. Go with a group when in doubt.

When walking, cross in the crosswalks, preferably at the lights.
- Orlando will fine you for jaywalking. I saw that happen.
- Honolulu used to fine you for texting while crossing the street on foot.
- The State of Washington will fine you for distracted driving, whether you're distracted by more than a mere glance towards your phone or by the food you're consuming.

I worked in downtown Columbus OH for one contract. The parking garage was across the street from work. There was a light right where I needed to cross the street to the parking garage.

However, that light was not at an intersection. This caused many drivers to not see that light. And, they didn't stop. I carried my rather large briefcase on the

Consulting 101
The Basics

traffic side of me. And, I swung it meaningfully towards anybody who looked like they weren't going to stop.

That was many years ago. And, I've grown wiser. Now, I would walk the extra ½ block down to the intersection and another ½ block back up to the parking garage, rather than demanding my rights via my briefcase.

For safety, I also escorted a female Consultant to that parking garage when we worked until midnight. It's not that women can't take care of themselves or that men can. It's just that muggers are more likely to attack a woman than a man. And, they're more likely to attack a person if they're alone.

Keep your wits about you.

Learn some self-defense techniques and strategies even if you don't believe in violence. Find an instructor who will teach you non-aggressive techniques. Self-defense includes feeling and looking confident, non-aggressive, and not an easy target.

Trust your sixth sense. If it tells you not to get onto an elevator or not to walk down an alley or to stay away from a certain person or group, do so. When you find out later that they're peace-loving monks, you can apologize to them.

I've worked in 15 different industries. Each one has their own safety standards. Various companies within an industry might have slightly different safety

Consulting 101
The Basics

policies. Some places at a Client might have stricter safety protocols than others.

As a Consultant, you'll need to follow the safety policies of both your Consulting Company and the Client. Normally, you'll be informed of those policies when they're different than just using common sense or if they involve wearing special equipment like hardhats.

Know the exit routes, both at your hotel and at the Client. Many Clients designate a few people as *Safety Monitors*. They will direct others on how to exit the building in case of an emergency – fire drill, etc. Follow their directions.

I stayed at a certain hotel in Toronto, Canada for several months on a Travel Assignment. That hotel occasionally had problems with their electrical equipment. And, that triggered their fire alarms on multiple occasions.

Luckily there was a Tim Horton's next door that was open all night. I could hang out there. Most of the people in the hotel hung out in the parking lot of the hotel that night. However, I thought it was too chilly for that. Then, again, I was used to a slightly warmer climate.

Consulting 101
The Basics

The Houseless

No doubt, you will run into the Houseless when you're in a larger city. They're also prevalent in some smaller cities. Houselessness is a problem that has existed for a long time.

In the US, many attribute that problem solely to drug use. But, there are other reasons why people are Houseless. I've heard that one of the main reasons that people are Houseless in the US is because they can't pay their medical bills.

The best way to prevent houselessness is to provide housing. I think that's best left to organizations and communities that have experience doing this. If you want to support the Houseless, that's probably best done by supporting an organization which is focused on them.

The Houseless need other services in addition to housing to help them be able to work and to have adequate health care and children's services. You might also consider supporting those organizations.

Consulting 101
The Basics

Often, the Houseless ask those who happen to be nearby for money. Why are they asking? You might wonder. Will they use that money for drugs or booze?

Some people give money to those who are playing music or to those who tell a good story. If you want to do this, it's wise to carry separate money for this in your pocket. That will allow you to easily pull it out without revealing how much money you're carrying.

Some people buy a fast-food meal and give it to the homeless.

If you feel strongly that you should give money to strangers asking for it, consider giving them local community currency when available. There's also Breadcoin. That's a bitcoin which is accepted at a few restaurants.

Alternatively, find an organization that helps the homeless. Then, make a donation to them.

Let me tell you about three homeless people who live near me.

The first, is an old man. Sometimes, he asks for money. But, his voice is weak. I know that my county is trying to offer the Houseless housing. So, why is he still living on the street?

I don't know. I have seen him in the grocery stores, buying groceries. He doesn't buy much. He only has a few coins. Still, it's food, not booze.

Consulting 101
The Basics

The second is a lady who's probably younger than we are. She sees us buying groceries all the time. We're walking. We are pulling our carts.

One day, she offered us a sack of groceries. But, we have different food requirements and wouldn't have been able to take it.

She explained that she had been given too much food that day. She only has one shelf where she can place her food where she lives.

People had been generous to her. She was being generous to us.

The third person, I read about in the paper. She lives in a homeless encampment. She wanted to start a garden. Even her best friends told her she was crazy. She got some tomato seeds and planted them. Next thing you know, she's growing tomatoes. Now, she feeds the entire encampment plus more from her garden. And, she grows all sorts of vegetables there.

Most Consultants are hardened to people who ask them for money. They avoid them when possible and ignore them otherwise. But, it should bother us to see so many people without a place to live.

Pope Francis says giving something to someone in need is always right and should be done with respect and compassion.

How you do that, I think, is up to you.

Consulting 101
The Basics

Making the World a Better Place

Making the World a Better Place for All

I wrote the previous chapter to let you know that you might encounter more Houseless on a Travel Assignment than you might in your home town. I did not write it to make you feel bad about not helping the Houseless enough.

I'm certain that *I* could do more to help the Houseless. Even so, my focus on making the World a better place for all is mostly elsewhere. It lies in helping people transform themselves and their lived environments. It lies in reminding people of Beauty, Wonder, and Paradise and how they can experience those things more easily.

There are many ways to make the World better. My focus is where my heart sings. My focus is where I've been headed for decades.

Most people do not have my focus. And, that's OK. IMHO, their focus should be on what makes *their* heart sing. It should be on what makes them look

Consulting 101
The Basics

forward to each day. It should be on what brings them joy.

    I could list various things that people focus on when they make the World better for all. Then, you could see which ones catch your attention.

    Sometimes, though, it's best to look at the World that's immediately around you. Look at yourself at the same time.

    What do you have in common? What strengths do you have that might offset your World's weaknesses? What beauty do you have to share that will bring beauty to your World?

Consulting 101
The Basics

Medical Needs

I am <u>not</u> a Medical Practitioner. I never even took Biology. Still, I can speak from personal experience.

Even the healthiest of us have medical needs from time to time. These might include dental appointments, colds, upset stomachs, headaches, and perhaps more serious ailments.

If you have sick-time, why not use it as needed? More than likely, it will expire if you don't use it. So you might as well use it, rest up, and stay refreshed.

Traveling while you're sick just sucks. Trust me.

If there's any way that I can avoid traveling when I'm sick, I do. Being sick while away from home also isn't any fun.

If I'm too sick to travel, I stay home. If I'm not too sick to work, I do so remotely.

The project can live without me for a few days. And, if it can't, they need to adjust the timeline.

Consulting 101
The Basics

I carry sore throat lozenges, vitamins, and herbs with me when I travel. I find that it's also a good idea to keep some facial tissues handy.

CleanWell[5] sells non-toxic sanitary wipes. Well, now, they're partnered with Seventh Generation who sells CleanWell branded as Seventh Generation. It will say CleanWell inside.

If you have a cold, you might want to wear a medical mask to protect others. That might also help you from reinfecting yourself.

Wearing medical and breathing masks is much less unusual now than it was when I was growing up. Some people wear a medical mask to protect themselves from others who might be sick.

Here in Hawaii, wearing medical masks is still common. It's becoming less common again in other parts of the US.

I still wear mine in crowded places. I will continue to do so even though I'm sometimes harassed for doing so.

It's a good idea to add your doctor, dentist, etc. to your phone contacts. It's also a good idea to let someone at work know if you're wearing a medical instruction tag.

---

[5] **CleanWell / Seventh Generation Partnership:** https://cleanwellinside.com/legacy-cleanwell/

Consulting 101
The Basics

If you need medical or dental treatment while away from home, consider which of the locals on the team think about their health needs in a similar way as you do. Then, ask them if they would mind giving you their doctor's or dentist's contact information.

You might also want to remember to contact at least one of your loved ones when you're sick. In some cases, you might want to have someone contact them for you.

IMHO, the best medical care is preventive care. This includes exercise. I try to walk and take the steps as much as I can. I also pack my luggage in two carry-ons and carry these through the airports. Two carry-ons are also easier to stow in the overhead or under the seat, than one carry-on and a roll-a-board. So, added bonus.

Preventive care also includes reducing stress. There are various methods to reduce stress.
- Deep breathing is one.
- Getting away from work, completely, is another.
- Letting your heart lead your mind into coherence is a third.[6]
- Unplugging from all electronic devices.
- Going for a stroll (not a power walk).
- Yoga.

---

[6] **Heartmath – Heart Coherence App and Exercises:** https://www.heartmath.com/

Consulting 101
The Basics

- Plants.

Pets can also help people de-stress. Nevertheless, you might not be able to take your pet into the Client site unless it's a certified service animal or perhaps, a plush animal.

Consulting 101
The Basics

Allergies and Sensitivities

I'm allergic to cut grass, broccoli, avocado peels, and wool. I deal with the latter three by avoiding them.

For cut grass, I chew on a mint leaf. It works for me. I carry mint leaves in case I run into cut-grass and start having trouble breathing, i.e. shortness of breath.

My wife has Multiple Chemical Sensitivities (MCS). This means that she's allergic or at least extremely sensitive to man-made chemicals.

For her, this is most noticeable in fragrances – perfume, laundry products, cologne, etc. Fragrances also negatively affect people with asthma. And, they give many people headaches and/or drain their energy. Sometimes fragrances cause people to have to go to the restroom frequently.

What my wife deals with is not fun, to say the least. This includes severe face pain, complete brain fog,

Consulting 101
The Basics

total lack of energy and more. At its worst these sensitivities leave her trapped at home.

However, she refuses to do that. She has found ways to protect herself when she needs to.

When I travel, I will more than likely pick up fragrances unintentionally. Sources include the aforementioned perfumes and colognes that other people are wearing and the fragrance of the laundry products that are still lingering on their clothes.

There's also the fragrances I pick up when I stay in hotels. When checking into a hotel, I call the local number. (This is not possible with some chains). Then, I ask the manager if I can get a fragrance-free room.

At Marriott hotels, I book Feather-Free rooms. That usually takes care of it.

You can find more tips on dealing with chemical sensitivities when traveling, by reading my book – Traveling with Multiple Chemical Sensitivities. You can also find resources for dealing with MCS at my website PrincessTigerLily.com/mcs.

Several Clients have policies against wearing heavy fragrance. I think it's just easier to avoid using fragrances, than to find out that they have such a policy once you're on site.

There are ADA (Americans with Disabilities Act) guidelines for providing a safe workplace for those with fragrance sensitivities.

Consulting 101
The Basics

The American Lung Association has a sample Fragrance-Free Policy on their website as does the Society for Human Resource Management.

OSHA (Occupational Safety and Health Administration) also guarantees workers the right to a safe environment. That includes being safe from fragrances.

Many people have allergies and/or sensitivities. There are common ones like dust, mites, feathers, pets, pollen, peanuts, and insect stings. Some are very rare, like my allergy to wool.

Some allergic reactions and sensitivities are mild enough that some people just ignore them. Some are more severe and yet people who have them might not recognize that they have them. For some people, they're very severe.

Consulting 101
The Basics

Conclusion
Is Consulting Right for Me? Should I wear that hat? Or, which hat should I wear?

Consulting Companies come in two modes – Consulting Companies and Staffing Firms.

Staffing Firms are more interested in placing you permanently with a Client.

Staffing Firms might place you on a Contract-to-Hire arrangement. Contract-to-Hire means that you're brought onto the project as a Consultant for three to six months. Then, the Client has the right to ask you to be an employee.

Consulting 101
The Basics

The Client doesn't have to hire you and you don't have to accept. Nevertheless, it's understood up front that if you're doing good work that the Client will offer you employment. And, it's understood that you will seriously consider their offer.

If you want to just try Consulting for a few months, try a contract-to-hire arrangement. If you end up liking Consulting, you can look for Consulting assignments that are not contract-to-hire arrangements when it's time for you to look for a new opportunity again.

On the other hand, you could try to land a short-term contract if you just want to check out Consulting.

One year on a Consulting project will be informative as to whether Consulting is right for you. Spending more than a few months on three separate projects for different Clients will let you make a more informed choice.

Consulting gives you an opportunity to work for one Company while gaining experience at several.
Consulting calls out the expert in you.
Consulting is a nice way to meet lots of people from around the world. And, Travel Assignments can take you to lots of places.

Consulting 101
The Basics

I thoroughly enjoy Consulting even though I'm not that personality type:

Meyer-Briggs ESFJ personality type is called the Consul or Provider – Extrovert Sensing Feeling Judging.

I'm an INFP – a Mediator or Idealist – Introvert, Intuitive, Feeling, Perceiving.

I encounter all sorts of personality types in my fellow Consultants. It takes many different personality types to make a good team and get the job done.

If you like working in different environments and meeting new people, you'll probably make a good Consultant. I'm considered more of an introvert because I often feel overwhelmed at social functions. At the same time, I get along well with most people.

It helps if you're self-confident, but not arrogant. People are relying on you to provide answers. Still, they don't want others showing them up.

You'll make a good Consultant if you don't let little things stand in your way. And, at the same time, you're willing to stand up for what's right.

Being an expert, being efficient, being very good at what you do, and being organized also helps.

You need to be a Team Player, not having to be in control, while still being able to direct others towards the best solution.

Consulting 101
The Basics

    Those are the things I've found that the best Consultants have in common.
    There are many lists of *What makes a good Consultant* on the internet. Those lists specify a lot of other attributes that might come in handy. Still, I've seen lots of Consultants get by without having them.

Consulting 101
The Basics

About the Author

    A good friend of mine (another Consultant) once told me that he didn't want to hear me complaining about how arduous my travel to the Client was.

    My travel included a connecting flight, two hours to the airport on my end, one hour to the airport on the Client's end.

    The reason why he didn't want to hear me complaining about my travel, was because I live in Paradise.

    And, I suppose I do.

Dale Stubbart

Consulting 101
The Basics

Just wait until I move to Hawaii. Then, I'll really have no excuse!

Update: Now, I do live in Hawaii! Luckily, my only Consulting Contracts while I've lived here have been fully remote. I would lose a day of work on each end if I had to be on-site in one of the other US states.

Still, most of those working on those projects and the Clients were located in the Eastern US Timezone. That's a six hour time difference. If they had wanted me to start at 8 am, their time, I would have had to start at 2 am, my time. I might have been able to do that in my younger years. But, I can't do that now. I know, I tried.

Luckily, they allowed me to start at 6 am, my time. This helped them out because they didn't have anybody else who was starting at noon their time and working until 7 pm or later.

Most of them left work at 3:30 pm or possibly 4:30 pm their time. I could easily cover those hours in my time zone.

We'll see what happens next. Will I retire? Will I get a local job as an Employee? Will I get another remote Consulting Assignment? Will I have to move from Hawaii to the mainland (the continental or contiguous states)?

Stay tuned!

Consulting 101
The Basics

Maybe, my books will make me rich enough that I won't have to worry about it.

Maybe, my Transformational Consulting will bring in some money.

Consulting 101
The Basics

Transformational Consultant

As a **Consultant**, I bring together my skills, expertise, and experience with those of my Clients, for the benefit of us both. By benefitting each other, the world gains an advantage and we all win.

Two heads are better than one, especially when one of those heads is mine. What can I say? Humility might not be my forte. Perhaps, it will be my eight-eh.

I am a Mystic at Home in the Sea of the Spiritual World. As a **Spiritual Consultant**, I'll help you find your Peace, Passion, and Paradise which are beyond any understanding or figuring out. I'll help you develop and enhance your relationship with the Loving Mystery.

I now refer to myself as a **Transformational Consultant.** Anyone, can benefit from being transformed. Whether you're spiritual or not.

Walking softly on my Mother Earth, I am at peace. As an **Earthwise Consultant**, I'll help you get in sync with your green lifestyle. I'll help you transform your lived environments. Together, we can renew the

Consulting 101
The Basics

Earth for future generations by meeting your sustainable triple-bottom line.

    Computers are second nature to me. As a **Computer or IT Consultant**, I'll help you use computers and data to communicate, stay organized, solve problems, and make your dreams of Paradise come true. Think of it as Computer Obedience Training from the Expert with more than 40 years of experience. Think of it as Computer Transformation.

    The Writing Muse found a willing partner in me for 130 Titles and counting. As a Writing, Editing, and Self-Publishing Consultant, I'll help you compose your thoughts into a story and your story into a book. I'll help you get your book self-published for the world to see. Leave your legacy and your legend for others to see. Touch the World while you also get your name in print.
    I'll help you transform your words, your story, your book.

Consulting 101
The Basics

Writer, Story Teller, Author

As an Author, I write stories in many categories [genres]. Often my stories include several categories.

Romance often accompanies **Fantasy**. **Fantasy** and **Science Fiction** are often combined. One of my books is a **Western Sci-Fi**.

You can find all of my books are on my website – Stubbart.com. There's a search box there to help you find what you're looking for.

My **Spiritual** books include:
- Spiritual Reference Books
- Mystical Writings
- Spiritual Fiction
- Fiction with a Spiritual Theme

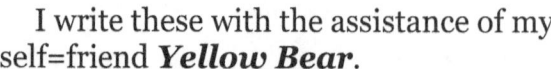

I write these with the assistance of my self=friend **Yellow Bear**.

My **Earthwise** books include books about:
- Living with Multiple Chemical Sensitivities

Consulting 101
The Basics

- Energy-Wise Transportation
- Other Topics

My Earthwise books can help you live according to your Earthwise lifestyle.

My **Computer** books are written to be easily understood, even if you have limited technical experience. In fact, about half of my computer books are non-technical in nature. That includes my book about a Robot who falls in love.

For my books in other genres, keep reading.

You'll find humor and romance in many of my books. I keep them clean, non-formulaic, and happy. Many of my books include poetry. Sometimes I include phrases and words from languages other than English. Yet they're still easy to read, even my reference books.

My books are far from boring, as my narrators and others have confirmed. To help in that regard, I keep my books concise, yet complete. As my wife says, I'm the only person she knows who can write a novel in a page. That might be a slight exaggeration.

I write stories that I would like to read. You'll find yourself right in the story. And you'll have an enjoyable journey all the way through, except for perhaps in some of my scary and lite-horror books.

My **Reference** books are informative, but not boring. They are stories, not just data, facts, and

Consulting 101
The Basics

figures. Delve into your preferred topic or choose to learn about something new. You'll find my **Reference** books among my **Spiritual**, **Earthwise**, and **Computer** books. My additional **Reference** books include books on **Food / Nutrition** and a **Tribute**.

If you would like to learn more about the computer work that I do, read my Reference book about **Consulting.** Oh, wait! That's this one!

I write Romance because I'm truly in love, just ask my wife. My **Romance** stories will speak to the true Romantic in you, the one who wants to love and to be loved. Let yourself be enamored again.

Children are some of my favorite people, no matter how old they are. My **Children's** stories will speak to the child in you. Let that happy baby come alive!

With Fantasies anything can happen and in my **Fantasy** stories it often does. Cheer on these protagonists as they live their unimaginably real lives in their impossibly real worlds. Get ready to be surprised with delight.

Fiction allows me to write what could happen. My **Fiction** stories allow you to consider alternate possible outcomes. What would the world be like, if …?

Outer Space, Aliens, Science Fiction intrigues me. These **Sci-Fi** stories will speak to the space-farer and

Consulting 101
The Basics

voyager in you. New worlds are out there waiting to be discovered by you.

I write Thrillers when I no longer want to run and hide. My **Horror** stories will help you face your fears. As Franklin Roosevelt said, *The only thing we have to fear is fear itself.* And at times, it can scare the $#@! out of me!

Consulting 101
The Basics

On the Outskirts of Paradise

In addition to living in Hawaii, **Dale Stubbart** and his wife now live on the *Outskirts of Paradise*. We live there, provided that we haven't forgotten for the moment where that is or what that's like. We try to allow ourselves to be happy and not get too bogged down by fear and rumors.

I can't speak for how my wife got here. However, *I* was certainly headed down the road to *Misery*, rather than the one to *Paradise*. However, something went awry. And, I kept being reminded of who I was and where I belonged.

Somehow, I remembered how to get back to Paradise. When I'm here, I remember how to help others recall what's important.

There are basically two ways to get to Paradise. You can enter by facing your fears and pains and allowing them to dissolve and be healed. Or, you can enter through joy and beauty.

Consulting 101
The Basics

You can rest assured that I will enter through joy and beauty 99 times out of 100. And, when you're willing, I'm willing to take you there with me.

Paradise is waiting for you. What are you waiting for?

Consulting 101
The Basics

Where I and my Books are on the Web

You can find all of my books on the Internet at Stubbart.com. With over 130 books, I'm certain you'll find something to your liking. Or my name's not **Dale Stubbart**.

On that website, you can browse for books by category. There's also a search box. Just enter a word that you want the book to be about and press submit. You can even enter a name. Enter ? for help on searching. Enter nothing to return a random set of books.

My other book about Consulting is <u>Solutions Galore</u>. It covers several methods of solving problems, some of which are uniquely my own.

You can find out more about my Transformational Consulting at Stubbart.com.

If you want to find out more about this thing I call Paradise, check out YellowBearJourneys.com.

Consulting 101
The Basics

All of my profile links are here:
https://stubbart.com/profile.html

Dale & Terry Stubbart

www.ingramcontent.com/pod-product-compliance
Lightning Source LLC
Chambersburg PA
CBHW070144230526
45471CB00002B/509